AF491769

I

CAN

MAKE

YOU

SUCCESSFUL

RIDHI CHANDA

Dedicated to: Maa Kali, for providing me with her energy to overcome every hurdle of life.

CONTENT PAGE:

Success is not built on success.
It's built on failure.
It's built on frustration.
It's built on fear.

Failure that you have to learn from.
Frustration that you have to swap
with focus.
Fear that you have to overcome.

INTRODUCTION

Hi! I'm Ridhi, currently pursuing my masters in Applied Mathematics at Indian Institute of Engineering Science and Technology. Now, the reason I have introduced my college and my course, so that I can address the elephant in the room, which is, I believe I'm the best possible author to pen down this book. I am a voracious reader, so I've read numerous books written on similar topics, watched vlogs and podcasts, followed youtube channels who make content related to this topic, but none was actually helpful. So basically, I've been there where you are now and that you have chosen to read this book.

My book shall address the doubts circumferencing "Success" in a cut-short, logical, simple and to-the-point manner. For the above reason, I intend to write a thin book and also use this font, cause, c'mon I am still a student, and I too hate books written in sophisticated fonts with minimal spaces and no pictures.

As a student of science, I love experimenting, and to be honest, I haven't even spared myself :)
So, this book is based on the case-studies that I have done on myself in the search of success.

Hope you have a happy reading :)

CASE STUDY-1

You know, as they say, the lines in your palm can never be changed or your fate is already destined. I would like to differ on this NOW, cause it is not true! With perseverance, practice and patience, one can achieve anything in life, though it may seem impossible at first.

You always wanted to know, what is that one thing that can lead you to success? The answer is simple: PERSEVERANCE.

Accha, okay, then what happens to the other virtues such as patience, hard work, and so on?
Then, my dear, you have to consider another physical constraint: TIME.

Needless to say, to achieve anything in life, it requires time and effort.
For how long should a person keep trying for a particular goal? Afterall, we cannot persevere for a lifetime for a particular goal.

To answer this question and many such questions, look at success just the way a scientist or a mathematician sees it.
When you ponder upon it, you'll come to this logical conclusion, that "Success" is nothing but "Cause and Effect".
You persevere (which is the cause) and then you succeed (which is the effect).

Coming back to our question, as to how long shall a person persevere?
The answer is again quite simple. For which you have to ask yourself two questions.

Do I need it in my life as much as I need
air to breathe? (The Burning Desire)
Does life seem impossible without it?

Question yourself while detaching
yourself from your goal, so that you
actually get your answers right.

If the answer is a "Yes", then my dear,
you will have to persevere unless and
until you achieve it. NOW, I do not mean
that you'll not use your intellect while
working hard or while building your
strategy, and that you'll continue to work
endlessly in the same direction for a
particular goal until you die.
Use your intellect, build strategies that
suit your working pace, have an informed
and proper direction to work on, and
persevere!

Trust me, you are now better than the others because you have figured out your "Why?"
You'll later get to know that even if you have begun late, but right, it will take you slightly less time than you thought, to accomplish it.
And, that, my dear, is the beauty of perseverance!

Coming to our time constraint. There is a particular time-period to achieve a particular goal. Here comes the different weapons. *Hard-work, consistency, patience, Smart-work, dedication, discipline,* and you name it.

First and foremost, come out of the illusion that smart-work can replace hard-work, and that smart-work is a better alternative to hard-work.

If your goal is big, and not everyone can achieve it, then you have to **work hard**. And I quote unquote what my mother always says, "There is no substitute for hard work". Trust me, it's hell true.

Out of all the weapons, and after a detailed analysis on this topic, keeping in mind that success is nothing but cause and effect, here is my conclusion. "Practice, Patience, and Perseverance" — The 3Ps you'll ever need.
All the other virtues which I have previously named, will fall under the 3 Ps.

Mathematician's tip: In this journey, there will be many small and big successes and failures. Analyze your failures, learn from it, make changes in your journey accordingly!

As Albert Einstein had said, "You cannot expect different results by doing the same things over and over again".

Make changes and *Practice*. I cannot emphasize enough on the fact that *Practice* is so important.
Practice with undivided attention is so important. It's simple, the more you practice, the better you become and the closer you get towards your goal.
One of the most important quotes that had a great impact in my life was of Sant Tukaram, "Aasadhiea te sadhiea karita sayas, kaaran abhiyas" ("I will practice over and over again and I will achieve it").
Practice.

If you have overworked yourself, and there's a lot of commotion going on inside your head, if you are unable to think properly and feel stagnant in life, I suggest that you should take a break.

The biggest mistake that I have made so far was not taking breaks at all. I had spent endless hours studying for days, weeks and even months without a break.
End Result?
Frustration.

Amidst your toil, do take healthy breaks, such as, go for a walk, have your favorite meal, or the simplest of all, take a nap!

If you are someone who actively uses social media:

→ Be mindful of what you watch online. Ek accha fighter, apna distraction bhi khud choose karta hai!
(A good fighter chooses his distractions as well!)

→ DO NOT! I repeat DO NOT fall into the loop of watching motivational videos aimlessly! Your brain loves getting the dopamine boost every time it is served with videos that provide you with instant gratification.

I hope you are still with me.

If not, I suggest you sit with a pen and paper and clear out your thoughts, including your ambitions, your strengths, your weaknesses, and most importantly, whether or not you are actually willing to make a change.

There will be a time when you won't be able to understand what actually is going wrong in your preparation. You have already tried and mapped out all the possibilities of improvement, still no visible progress.
Trust me, you are mentally exhausted.
You need a break.

You know I have made a theory and I call it "*The Circumference Theory*". Here, your goal is at the center of the circle and you are working hard inside the circle to converge to your goal. Now, you distance yourself from the center of your goal, and observe it from its circumference. You can call it, to have a Bird's Eye View. You'll get to see the goal

and the path or the trajectory you have
taken to achieve it. That way, you
yourself will be able to judge whether or
not you'll achieve it.

Meaning, You take a day off, or two, or
it's even healthy to take a week off. Do
not feel guilty of providing yourself with
a break according to your needs. Take
the much-needed break, relax your body
and mind, have a great meal, go out for a
small excursion, sleep well, or do what I
do, play, play badminton or football or
any other sport of your choice.

Now I suppose you believe me when I say
that I am the coolest and the most
logical author this generation will ever
earn! JK :)
I could have said that for all generations
but then I remembered I have to be
logical too. My bad!

Anyways, yes, coming back, relax as much as you can. Now, the most important part, when you'll be left with 30% of your break-time period, then you just simply observe your goal (the center) from its circumference. Observe it casually. Observe it being a third person. Suggest some changes (if any) regarding your preparation, as you would suggest someone else having the same preparation as you.
My dear, befriend yourself :)
Have healthy conversations with yourself, just as how friends usually have, well, good friends usually have.

DO NOT! I repeat DO NOT continuously accuse yourself of not completing the targets. Trust me, it's okay! It's completely natural!

You are a human, not a machine! Listen to your body. Do not overwork your body or your brain.
Start slow and navigate through your problems, reach its root-cause, and then take necessary actions, again by starting slow.

Observe your goal from the circumference, regain energy, regain the mindset, believe that you can, and then when you will move towards the center, the world shall know that you have won the world at the center.

This is because you had patience. You were patient with yourself and your work. You gave yourself the much needed time to be back to the game, but with more clarity this time.

You made it!

You made it, because you worked hard for it (*Practice*), not only that, you stood up again and again after every fall (*Perseverance*), and you had *patience*, patience with yourself and your work. You persevered without bothering much of the outcome.

Wait! Wait! Wait!
Ridhi, is not the love for the subject or the love for the work solely enough to make us work hard for our goals?

Umm, tbh not enough!
Look, initially it helps. But we need to remember that any goal on this planet is not only a bed of roses, it is covered with thorns too.
Subject-wise speaking, there will be some topics of your favourite subject too which will not be your favourite!

There for a few minutes, the love for the subject just effaces off our minds. And when you have a bigger goal in life, like becoming a billionaire one day, you have to do many things which you don't enjoy much, like saying no to every hang-outs with friends and rising up after every fall.

At those times, my friend, the 3Ps will come to your rescue!

CASE-STUDY 2

Now, if you think that, it is a lot!
Trust me, it's not!
You know why?
Because your focus is at the wide
distance between you and your goal, and
on the fact that you have to do a lot of
things, and along with you, many have
already read this book, and the pressure
of starting your preparation soon...
Zzzzzzzzzzzzz...
Cut the crap!
Babe, you are overwhelmed!

Suno,
Apni nazar sirf apne aagle kadam pe he
rakhna hai!
Aur 3Ps ki talwar leke aage badna hai.
Bss!

(Keep your focus solely on your next step
and follow the 3Ps).

You have to keep your focus on:

- ★ Today's practice.

- ★ Whether or not, you are rising up
  after every fall (Perseverance).

- ★ Whether or not you are patient
  with yourself and your work.

As a young mathematician, I guess I can
call myself that, after hours of research
on various mathematical, scientific and
on AI/ML topics, (IK, IK I'm still unsure
to call myself a mathematician and it may
seem like I'm seeking validation or
something :))

Woh kya hai na ki science student hu, toh
koi bhi credit ki aadat nahi hoti hamhe,
aur jitna bhi karlo, kam he hai!

So, as a mathematician, I have read many
books. I mean, many!
Interestingly, the world's most scientific
and logical book is present at our
homes— The Bhagavad Gita.

Lord Krishna, the param Guru, said it and
still continues to say it, only if we could
become a little more attentive.
Bhagavad Gita se khaas aaj aapke liye,
"Do not focus on the outcome! Keep your
focus on your karm (work), and continue
to work with undivided attention".

Plain and simple Babe.
When you keep your focus on your karm,
then trust me the Case-Study 1 is much
simpler.

When you keep your focus on your karm,
then I suppose, you don't know any such
thing as "Fear of Failure"!

CASE-STUDY 3
LUCK

You know what people think about luck? It often happens to be that, when a successful woman sits in the dining table with a woman who's pursuing success, the latter narrates the difficulties that she faced and is still facing, along with many uncertainties, then probably leading to a rant about the process, about the system, and about the management, although these may not be completely false. Then she ends her rant saying,"You achieved it soon. You were lucky!"

There is never a comparison between the struggles of two people.
We do not know whose starting line was much behind.

I believe every person has to go through their own set of struggles. Then where was the difference between her and the successful woman?

Probably, the perspective towards struggle.

When we are in our struggling phase, because of the intensity of our adversities, we tend to think that the person who recently achieved his/her goal, had to face less challenges. I have been on both sides of that dining table. So trust me when I say this, the one who has achieved her goal, started working for it long before you have. She has faced equal or more rejections and self-doubts than you have, as we need only one person to cut the mountain, then the rest can struggle just to walk through it. Trust me, she has been in the ocean of uncertainties much longer than you have.

Take for example this book. The person reading this book, probably will gain clarity faster than it took for me to gain. So, come out of the denial phase, the successful person, irrespective of class (if he is from a well-to-do family, then he will have an easier access to so many distractions) was lucky, although he worked hard, because once you think this, then there is nothing left to work upon. Eventually you'll tend to give up early and easily.

You know, people also say that if someone is successful, then it was her 99% hard work and 1% luck.
Well, logically, I cannot rule out the 1%. Afterall, a mere epsilon is given so much

importance in mathematics, which is
much much smaller than 1%.
The 1%, I give credit to
butterfly-effect.

Butterfly-Effect is a concept, which says
that small changes can have far-reaching
and unpredictable consequences.
The idea is that the flap of a butterfly's
wings in one part of the world could
potentially set off a chain of events
leading to significant impacts elsewhere.
Mind you, it is a scientific concept, which
is clearly based on the concept of "cause
and effect". It also explains the fact
that everything in this universe is
connected. If there is a cause in one end,
then there will be an effect too because
of it.
For instance, let us consider that you
have worked extremely hard for your
exams and also followed the 3 Ps, and you

do have the capabilities of getting a rank 1, but the morning you are leaving for your exams, the bus got late due to xyz reasons, and you reached the examination center late. You are late by 35 minutes and now there are cortisol secretions in your body and because of it there is a lot of panic. So, the probability of you making mistakes in the exam increases, and the probability of you getting rank 1 decreases.

So, because of an unavoidable cause, the after-effects change drastically. This phenomenon is called "The Butterfly Effect".

Boys and Girls, you constantly look for answers even after having one, thinking that you might have missed on something because of which you aren't able to succeed, but that's not true!

I have been there and I very well know
this phase.
I have researched a lot for the answers
highlighted in this book, from various
speeches of important people, and even
read various books on this topic, but none
seem to actually satisfy my soul.

Do you know, what is the one thing that
Nature or the Universe cannot take away
from you?
The will to try! Again!

By perseverance, you can increase your
probability of winning.
Find out your weaknesses, and
"repeatedly try" to improve them, then
none can stop you from achieving your
goals.

A slight detour :)

You see, when I was little, I was told
that I would never excel in life and would
never get above 80% if I choose any
analytical subject, like Mathematics,
Science, Computer-Science.
In fact, the Astrologer told me that I
should take up English and Social
Studies, so that I could get a higher
percentage.
As usual, I was fascinated by his
prediction, and wanted to experiment.
That was in class 6. In the following
years, I scored above 95% in
mathematics and scored the highest
(100%) in the whole state in my SSC
Examinations, although I did score the
highest in English as well that year
(86%). In Science I scored 95%.
Went on and took up mathematics as my
honors paper in my bachelors degree, and

currently, pursuing masters in Applied Mathematics at Indian Institute of Engineering Science and Technology.

I do have big ambitions and it still gives me immense happiness in not taking other people's opinion as an ultimatum, but to experiment and find out the actual results.

So basically, according to the astrologer or maybe even according to the lines in the palm of my hand, mathematics was not for me. To be honest, I am not someone who is "gifted" or something and it wasn't luck, because I didn't win once. I won every time I followed the 3Ps. It was pure practice.
A hell lot of practice.
Perseverance.
Patience.

At present, my health condition is bad, and even after many achievements, I have now hit the rock bottom, once again. Trust me, I have never fallen this low in life. Sitting in my hostel room, all alone, I didn't go to write my mid-semester examinations, because I am unable to hold a pen, because of my shaky hands and feet, due to the higher doses of my medication.

So, to be honest, I just wanted to see whether I can actually use this time productively and once again, thought of experimenting.

And see, I am able to type :)

Let's say this just as how people would have told me,

"You are able to type. You are indeed lucky, Ridhi !"

Well, they are not able to feel the pain that I'm going through right now, nor do they know the back story. Interestingly, they told me that I was really lucky that writing a book was included in my fate.
Lol.

So, what do you think about luck now?

And people's opinion?
Still matters?

TAKE-AWAYS

→ Your company matters a lot. It is far better to be alone than to be in a bad company.

→ Whenever extremely stressed out, reach out to your support system, that can be anyone, your parents, friends, who without a second thought, wants you to make progress.

→ Take care of your body. Your health is of utmost importance. Don't want to spare much time on it?
Do Yoga for 20 minutes a day (Surya Namaskar is mandatory)
And 10 minutes practice awareness (meditation or deep breathing).

You see, if you actually passionately love the preparation phase, the learning and making mistakes phase, trust me, you are truly worthy of achieving your goals!

CASE-STUDY 4
BELIEVE

This is the most important case study as compared to all the previous ones.
Then why is it towards the end of this book?
Well, unfortunately, that's how I discovered it in my journey towards success!
The most important weapon. At the last.

Anyways,
Once my Astrologer told me that I am an atheist!
I was shocked. Me? Atheist?
I am writing a book dedicated to Kali Maa. C'mon man!

In olden times, an atheist means a person
who does not believe in God. But now,
time has changed! Atheist is someone
who does not believe in himself.

The crux of the matter is, I never had
immense belief in the fact that Yes, I
can make it! I too can be successful and
that definitely this time I'm gonna make
it!

Now this may seem to be a very simple
factor, but it is not!
If you strongly believe in yourself, you
can even move mountains!
Yes! Mountains!
Such strong is the power of belief!

Do you remember the story of Dashrath
Manjhi? His wife was injured and needed
immediate medical attention. However, a
massive mountain stood between the

village and the town. Tragically, she died due to the delay.

Devastated by her death, he decided to carve a path through the mountain, so that no one else should suffer the same. For 22 long years, he single-handedly worked on cutting through the mountain. That seemed impossible for almost everyone, to even think of it, but he did it.
He believed in himself that he could carve a path, and so he succeeded.
Such immense belief he had in himself.

You know, nothing in fact is present in this world that is not achievable. You can achieve anything!

There are no set rules or boundations to achieve a particular goal. You are not bound by anything. You can achieve any

goal you want! You have that capability
within you! Literally everything is
possible!

You have to have immense belief within
you that even if the Universe tests you
multiple times (adversities of life), your
belief should not be shakeable!
And if you dare to rise up every time you
fall, then trust me, nothing can stop you
from achieving your goal.

These things that I'm saying are not at
all "Motivation"!
When you'll actually feel this way
towards your goal, then trust me, the
next time you try, you will be successful!

Cause I have felt it and the next time I
tried, I succeeded.
I have also researched this "Believe", and
all the important men and women in this

world had this "Believe" within themselves.

In Scientific terms, this comes under the concept of "Placebo Effect". If you believe you can do it, then eventually you will be able to do it!

That's it. You are good to go.

All the very best, dear friend!

Let me know your experiences through emails, then I'll believe that I could help someone out there who was burdened with questions and was unsure of his/her next step, as I was, a few years ago.

<u>CASE-STUDY 5</u>
<u>SUCCESS</u>

When you'll achieve your goals with all
your senses open, you'll feel nothing!
You'll feel a void inside your heart.
There'll be a sense of relief in your eyes.
You'll know that you deserved it!

Then you'll realize that you have not done
anything extraordinary, in fact, you did
the ordinary things, the extra times.
You'll realize that the success you've
achieved is just a mere "effect" of the
"cause" that you've put in.
You'll realize that anyone, literally anyone
can achieve anything in this world.
You'll realize that you can achieve
anything in this world.

You'll be filled with satisfaction and a
deep sigh!
You won't feel any butterflies in your
stomach, or the feelings that are shown
in televisions.

This satisfaction after toiling hard for a
long period of time is itself happiness.

While accomplishing your life through
difficult jungles and high mountains,
When you'll win the last peak too,
When you'll feel there is no difference
left, between you and the roughness of
those mountains that you have won
When you'll bear the first storm of ice
on your forehead, and you'll not tremble,
Then you'll find that there is no
difference in winning everything,
and *not giving up till the end.*

A small note for you, my dear Reader:

In this vast growling ocean of life, your
failures will be the rudders of your boat,
and will take you a long way in life.
Dear Reader, do not be afraid to fail!
Give yourself the permission to fail!
Trust me, you don't have to figure out
life all at once. Take your time to unlearn
things, explore and learn new things.

There's a lot in common between you and
me, and I would like to believe that
you're a lot more brave than me, cause
life really scared the hell out of me many
times.
But no worries, I have your back now.
Hope you succeed in all your endeavours,
and I'm rooting for you, always :)

More power to you, friend!
Wishing you all the success in life!

ACKNOWLEDGEMENTS

This book is an outcome of all the nooks
and corners I had bumped into, in those
dark lanes, in search of success.
So yeah, if not for all those missed
opportunities, those failures, those
hurdles in life, then I would not have
been able to share my experiences
through the case studies in this book.

As it is said, "Our greatest glory is not in
never failing, but in rising everytime we
fall".

This book is for those comebacks that
I've made, for those little strengths and
courage I had to once again stand up in
those gloomy times, with no one by my
side, encouraging me.
You know what? Thank God, I stood up!
Again! Phew!

I thank those hurdles in life that pushed
me to get up everytime I fell.
At that time, it felt terrible, but
eventually it was all worth it!

ABOUT THE AUTHOR

Well, nothing much about me to be honest. My name is Ridhi. I am a student, pursuing masters in Applied Mathematics at Indian Institute of Engineering Science and Technology.
A to-be mathematician, who loves experimenting including with her own beliefs.

This is my first ever book which I have penned after struggling a lot with "Success" in life.
Just a simple wish with which I have put words through the pages of this book is to help out that one mind which is burdened with a lot of questions on "Success".

Connect with me at:
ridhichanda755@gmail.com